The Challenge of Brazil

Letters and Events recounted by Sister Katey Dougan and compiled by Father Kenneth Payne

An environmentally friendly book printed and bound in England by www.printondemand-worldwide.com

FSC
Mixed Sources
Product group from well-managed forests, and other controlled sources
www.fsc.org Cert no. TT-COC-002641
© 1996 Forest Stewardship Council

PEFC
PEFC/16-33-416
PEFC Certified
This product is from sustainably managed forests and controlled sources
www.pefc.org

This book is made entirely of chain-of-custody materials

FastPrint Publishing

www.fast-print.net/store.php

THE CHALLENGE OF BRAZIL

A catalogue record for this book is available from the British Library

ISBN 978-178456-101-7

First published 2014 by
FASTPRINT PUBLISHING
Peterborough, England.

Table of Contents

Acknowledgements.

I am most grateful for the comments and corrections suggested by the following:

Sister Katey's family, The St. Louis Sisters, Lana Murphy, Catherine Chappell, Michelle Gibbins, Lorna Foort, the quotations from Clodovis Boff's book 'Feet-On-The-Ground-Theology' (Orbis Books, Maryknoll, New York, 1987), and the front cover picture by Elda Broïlo, used with permission.

Introduction

Letter writing is fast becoming a lost art, being killed by the internet, text messages, Twitter and Facebook. It was with nostalgia and renewed interest that I discovered in a drawer a bundle of letters, written over a period of several years. They were from a friend, Sister Katey Dougan, who had been engaged in missionary work in Brazil for over twenty years. These coupled with a previously published account of a visit I had made to see her in Brazil, gave me the impetus to share her thoughts as well as my own.

Katey Dougan, a Saint Louis sister, spent a number of years helping the poor and needy and by her life spreading the Good News of the Kingdom in Brazil. I have in most cases retained the conversational style of writing adopted by Katey in her letters, as this helps to bring alive her experiences.

Much of what follows finds an echo in Pope Francis' published 'Exhortation' 'The Joy of the Gospel', in which he was clearly influenced by his own ministry in South America, and by liberation theology. He has close ties with the Church's social practices and in particular its concern for the poor. Similar problems have since occurred in Europe: the problem of keeping the Christian faith and practice alive in the absence of clergy. Pope Francis has said that we must have 'a poor church for the poor'. I have taken the liberty of developing this theme much as it occurs in Clodovis Boff's book, 'Feet on the

Ground Theology' published in 1984. This is a record of his five months spent mostly in the Amazon jungle. His theory and experiences influenced Sister Katey in what follows of her work in Brazil.

Chapter 1: Brazil

Brazil has been frequently in the news with the World Cup 2014 and the Olympic Games on the horizon for 2016. However it would not be true to say that Brazilians all play football, dance the samba and enjoy an endless summer!

It is larger in area than the whole of Europe but with a population of over 200 million. In the cities, like Sao Paolo and Rio De Janerio there is a stark contrast between the high rise office and hotel blocks and the favelas, the slum dwellings sandwiched between them. In many of the country areas there is less contrast as most of the people are poor and live in shacks. In many parts of the Brazilian jungle the main highway in the hot weather becomes more like a donkey path, partly overgrown and eroded by the rain. Life for those living in the jungle can be very hard and most are on the poverty line: rubber gatherers, washer women, servants and a few small merchants.

Brazil's patron Saint is Nossa Senhora Aparacida, a black Madonna, appropriately so as half the population are black or mixed race. Brazil has peaceful relationships with its neighbours, but paradoxically violence is rampant within the country where there is such a great contrast between the rich and poor. Up to 50 thousand people are murdered every year.

The church in Brazil, and especially in the country areas, is one where you really feel the Spirit of Christ, where there is Christian joy and fellowship and love amongst its members. To be a pastoral worker, a sister or a priest requires great courage and determination, as the conditions, especially in the jungle and poorer areas, are very hard. There are countless examples of the church functioning in its mission *for* the poor but only in certain areas is it a church *of* the poor, and very rarely a poor church. Clodovis Boff in his book writes

"The whole point is to see if this 'for the poor' is heading toward becoming 'with the poor' so that it will eventually become an 'of the poor'. This is a historical process that advances by a twofold movement, the church coming closer to the poor and becoming identified with them and the poor emerging within the church as ecclesial agents. This is the option for the poor and for the poor as leaders – at first potentially and then in reality. 'Church of the poor' is both an ideal and an emerging process"

However, on a more optimistic note it is very often the poor who are giving evidence of the presence of the Kingdom of God here and now. There are times when the poor are embarrassed by their poverty, but in fact the opposite should be true: we should be embarrassed by our relative prosperity. Boff later continues

"One young man had been waiting in the endless line at the gas station from 4 am until 3pm. Eleven hours in line. Only then could he get a gallon of diesel fuel, and that was what we were using. He didn't make a fuss about his long wait. He scarcely mentioned it. And others weren't surprised. But I was very impressed: waiting a whole day for a gallon of fuel. "You didn't eat?" I asked him. "No – otherwise I'd lose my place in line". He didn't talk like someone who thought he'd been wronged. No question about it, what the ordinary people have to suffer goes unheard. They don't have anyone to complain to, unlike the upper classes who, at the least inconvenience, have the public media to blare out their complaints. Poverty and suffering go together like twins. And the poor suffer not only from the nonsatisfaction of biological needs, but also from moral injustices, humiliation, pressure, oppression, persecution."

We are reminded of the life of Jesus. He was born poor, lived poorly, possessed nothing and died as one rejected by his own people. He enjoyed no privileges or titles and often had nowhere to lay his head. However, it is true to say that, for us, being poor, we become less frenzied and preoccupied with the trivia of life. Do we in fact find the poor happier and more joyful: the joy of the Gospel?

The shortage of priests is paramount throughout Brazil and in consequence training courses are most important for lay leaders. Sometimes these pose a problem as it is not always possible to attend them. Excuses are sometimes made: distance to go and work with the rubber. However when these difficulties are overcome there is great enthusiasm. Often a priest is involved, not as a leader, but just present, giving guidance when necessary. Lay leaders, when properly trained become the pillars of a community. The training often involves looking in detail at the life of the early church as recounted in the Acts of the Apostles. This involves fidelity to the word of God, a community of possessions, the breaking of bread and prayer and above all, joy.

Leaders come together regularly to share and to give support to one another.

"If we live by the truth and in love we shall grow completely into Christ, who is the head by whom the whole Body is fitted and joined together, every joint adding its own strength for each individual part to work according to its function. So the Body grows until it has built itself up in love" (Ephesians 4, 16).

This leads me to include a few remarks about the importance of community, although in some ways this is hardly necessary as community is integral to the lives of Brazilians living especially in the country areas. The Sacraments, Baptism and Marriage, only make sense if they grow out of a living faith community. Groups with lay leadership meet regularly and are always a part of the bigger grouping of the parish. Where possible they have their own centre. Coordinators at all levels bring together the leaders. Ideally the clergy and pastoral workers should live in community and even share the life of the people they serve, although this is seldom the case. In this the Eucharist is all-important and it can be celebrated in so many different ways, from being seated on the ground with the table cloth spread out in front of the priest and the bread and wine necessary for the Mass, or more formally with shared prayers of intercession and offertory procession, and with the sign of peace to break the ice at the beginning of the Mass. Perhaps it would also be desirable, although it is not at present happening, to have a priest coming from the local community and ordained as the 'presbyter' just for that community. A priest once said that you feel most frustrated when you don't find happiness and fulfilment in your work with people. If that doesn't happen, you can regard yourself as the biggest failure in the world. This can happen to anyone. There is a joy in service. This is the joy of the Beatitudes, and the joy of celebrating the Eucharist.

Pope Francis sums up all this admirably in his Exhortation. "In all places and circumstances, Christians, with the help of their pastors, are called to hear the cry of the poor. This has been eloquently stated by the bishops of Brazil: 'We wish to take up daily the joys and hopes, the difficulties and sorrows of the Brazilian people, especially of those living in the barrios and the countryside – landless, homeless, lacking food and health care – to the detriment of their rights. Seeing their poverty, hearing the cries and knowing their sufferings, we are scandalized because we know that there is enough food for everyone and that hunger is the result of a poor distribution of goods and income. The problem is made worse by the generalised practice of wastefulness'. (Paragraph 191)".

So with these thoughts in mind, I now invite the reader to come down to earth with some of Sister Katey's experiences of her ministry in Brazil.

Chapter 2: Off to the Mission

On our journey in the morning from Heathrow, another sister and myself got through without having to pay for our excess luggage, which was a great relief. We were delayed one hour leaving London so had only just time in Amsterdam to walk the long passageway to get to our plane. The flight in the jumbo took twelve hours and we arrived 9am local time and 12 midnight G.M.T.

It was warm and sticky when we arrived in Rio and with all the dealings with the Federal Police and luggage we didn't go through the barriers until 11pm. We were met by Sister Anne and Fr. John, a local priest working in a parish in Rio. We stayed at his house and the next day he gave us a quick tour of Rio on our way, yet again, to the airport. It was Carnival time so everything was closed and everybody seemed to be at the beach. As well as the famous sights of Rio we saw some favelas – huts just stuck in the side of the mountain – such a contrast to the prosperous parts we had seen.

We got to the airport to find that our flight to Forania had been cancelled. Anne, who is excellent at the language, got them to read the small print and said that it was their responsibility to put us on a flight. This they did, but via San Paulo, where we had a two hour delay before catching another plane to Forania. We arrived there at 11pm and got a taxi out to our house. We were an hour's ride from the centre of the city and then for the next two days we had to travel out to get our papers with the police and more photos taken. There are just two in the community there, one of whom is Brazilian. The heat and the crowded houses were breathtaking. In the parish we saw a small group of washerwomen and one man learning how to read and write. There was great rejoicing as one woman, for the first time, wrote her name.

On Saturday we set off at 7pm for our journey by bus southwards and arrived in Barrolandia the next morning at 9.30am. The journey can take up until 1pm but the driver didn't waste any time throughout the night. The bus was crowded and had no air-conditioning. Barrolandia was our first community in Brazil and since its foundation it has changed greatly. The main street is a huge wide dirt road with some cement houses although they are mainly made of mud. When we arrived there 12 years ago the people just said "You are a sign of hope for us". We have a health post here now and are in charge of the parish. Sister Anne has just finished her term of 6 years and is going to Colmeia at the end of her stay. Judy, an American, has taken over from her.

On Sunday evening we went to "Ito Mass of the Irma", the sisters' Mass as they say locally. The church was half filled, mainly women, and there was great singing. We two new sisters were welcomed and given a round of applause and afterwards all came to welcome us individually. This is a time when you miss out on the language. I went with Anne the next evening, during a great thunder storm, to visit some families. One house just had a mud floor but was spotlessly clean. The Brazilians always offer you a cup of coffee which is very sweet "a cafezinho". It is certainly a man's world here, the women do most of the work and the girls get married, some as young as 12 years of age. At our house people come and go all the time. An old lady who is 83 comes every day just for a chat. She thought we looked lovely and pale. Most of them are dark skinned but others quite pale by Brazilian standards.

My journey still was not over. The second part was by car to Colmeia. The highway from south to north is mainly straight and to either side vast stretches of land, some parts of which are heavily wooded with palms. We drove by Volks. from Barrolandia to Colmeia and that took three hours, as Colmeia is an hour's journey west of the highway and up on a hill. In the distance there are beautiful mountains and some lovely views. Until two years ago there was only a dirt road there which was really treacherous. Electricity also came two years ago and water is erratic, although fortunately for the past six months we have a supply. The main street of the town looks good and the road tarmacked, but off that are dirt roads. There are about 10,000 people in the town with many surrounding communities.

Margie is in charge of the parish and on Sunday we will be having our first Mass since Christmas Eve celebrated by a local Brazilian priest. Yesterday I went visiting a part of the town where there is great poverty. In one hut lived a mother, separated from her husband, with her seven children and her parents. There is a lot of prostitution all over Brazil and the small villages are no exception. On Friday we went north by car – three hours to Araguania to check in with the Federal Police and get our identity cards. This process took all day. We went to the bank and then to the police and back to the bank. Time is of the essence here.

It is the rainy season so we have had some terrible thunderstorms; they however cool the atmosphere for a short time. July and August is the very hot season. The plants are beautiful, now that the rains are here, and last night it was lovely seeing all the fireflies light up the bushes. Fruits too are plentiful, all tropical. We headed south to Brasilia after my meeting in Muricilomdia. In fact we are 20 hours from Brasilia and 20 hours by bus from Belem in the north. We are in what is called the lower Amazon basin between the two rivers Araguaia and the Tocantins.

Since we have come the money has changed, three noughts have been removed so a 10,000 becomes 10, very confusing for newcomers and a big blow for the poor. The collection in Barrolandia last Sunday was less than two dollars, just a few cruzados and yet to see these people wanting to give something just stays with you: truly the widow's mite.

We are divided into groups here and take responsibility for different aspects of the community life. Last week I was on liturgy and that was really good. Because we have a mixed group: we have ecumenical services, and on Friday it was led by the Methodist padre and the rest of our group. He and his wife are in my small language group and are really a fine couple. We have six married couples in the school, Lutheran and Methodist, and all of them are German. One couple has a young baby of five months, and another couple have two children aged four and two and they have picked up the language with no trouble. They go to a nursery school nearby.

I can't believe that I've only one month left here in Brasilia. We finish on 23rd June. The language is difficult and some days are better than others. At the beginning of May I spent ten days with a Brazilian family in Goiania, which is four hours by bus from here. They were a young couple with a three year old son and the granny living in the same compound. The family were just super. On the first day, Sunday, I had to stand up and introduce myself in Church and after Mass all came to welcome me. Half the time I didn't have a clue what was being said and I don't know who said yes to me. The "Yes" came after I'd ask them to say it a second time and when I didn't get what they said I just nodded and said "Yes!" The granny and her family next door heard of my arrival and so all came to the house with their families and I met so many people. I went to meetings in the Church, visited the sick, ate with the neighbours, played the guitar in the folk group and learned how to make lovely yeast bread, Brazilian style.

This weekend 3rd June we have a reunion with our families. People on the course here went to different parts of Brazil – some as far away as six hours by bus. Then some just went to the outskirts of the city. We have a community in Goiania so it was great that I was assigned near there as I hope to keep in contact with the family I had stayed with. Ten of us went to Goiania and we returned on Saturday to visit our families. While there, Marie Lucia, mother of my family, took me to visit her niece, a fifteen year old, with a new baby a few days old, and recently married to a fifteen year old lad. She looked about eleven years old and her house was dreadful: they lived in two tiny rooms.

In April we had a terrible shock. One of the French priests was found dead in his room. He died in the night of his 56th birthday. He had been in great form and hadn't shown any signs of illness. His body had to be flown back to France, simply because the three priests were coming for the first time to Brazil to work, and after the course hoped to find a suitable place and therefore did not have a base here. It was really sad and put language learning into perspective.

We have classes each morning from 8am till 12, and now in the afternoons we have lectures on the history and geography and every aspect of life in Brazil. Some weeks ago we had a special week of prayer for the Indians and looked at the whole area of Brazil and the political implications for the government. The government here did not like the international coverage it was getting.

Two Sundays ago I went with the director of the course, for Mass out to a favela - one of many in the outskirts of this very modern city. It is unbelievable the conditions there, no running water, and the houses are just constructed of pieces of wood with a plastic roof. A couple of us went walking around the favela as we had plenty of time before Mass. One lady invited us into her home, just a clay floor and tiny partitions for each bed. It was Mothers' Day so her daughters were there with their babies. At Mass that evening in a makeshift classroom, all arrived with beautiful flowers and put them in vases. We had a candlelit procession to begin the Mass, and the Bible was carried in by a young mum. At the end of Mass each mother was given a tiny paper flower.

Chapter 3: Colmeia: 1990

The elections are coming up on Wednesday 15th and the school will be closed this week in preparation for them. All the campaigning is going on and we have been trying to arouse people's consciences regarding the importance of voting, not actually saying the name but helping people as so many people here cannot read or write, especially here in the interior. One of the candidates we would definitely be in favour of, happens to be the first one on the ballot paper and that means that the people will not have the problem of reading down the whole list. Most could not even read the names.

About three weeks ago I spent a week with a Brazilian community in a place called President de Kennedy which is about two hours north of here. There were three sisters in the community and seven pre-postulants, so you can imagine I had every chance to get to know the language. Also to get to know the Brazilian reality from the Brazilian view point, rather than from the 'estrangeires' as they say here, the 'foreigners'. So I spent the week there and took part in the life of the community: prayer, up very early in the morning and then went visiting the sick in the area, also visiting two communities in the Sertao, which means the interior of Brazil. We left at 8 o'clock in the morning and arrived back about 7 o'clock in the evening. The first day we went on the Friday and we were to meet the youth at nine, having had lunch, but they finally came about a quarter to eleven. This is nothing new in Brazil. Word gets out when you arrive and then they start coming, they don't wait for you to come. They only start arriving later on. So first of all we had the youth meeting, about fifteen of them, and some of them had walked miles to get there.

We met in a little barraca - a kind of palm leaf hut which was nice and cool inside. As the day went on it got really hot but we had filtered water which was good, and I kept running to it every so often. We had the meeting and then people started arriving, because in the afternoon there were to be baptisms and weddings. So the people started coming about 12 to 1 o'clock and then someone went and brought our lunch. All these pots, a pot of chicken, chicken pieces, and that means feet as well. They eat the whole works here: chicken, rice, beans and pequi. These look like conkers and people here use them to flavour the rice. I love them – they have a very strong flavour, but some do not like them. At the moment I eat everything that is going. I like to experiment with all the new types of food. Speaking of that, they have fantastic varieties. They really have everything but the sources are just not tapped. The older people here can give you a remedy for snake bites, all kinds of chas which are teas, and there are calmantes for calming the nerves. When I was in Kennedy I brought back some of their little plants, to plant here.

After lunch more people arrived and everybody was invited to have lunch although most people came having had theirs. We have our lunch here every day at quarter past eleven in the morning. So most people will have had their lunch when they came. At about two or half past two, we had baptisms. In fact we only had two and then we had a wedding and the wedding was the religious ceremony. They have two ceremonies here, one civil and one religious. A lot of people cannot afford the civil one because it is so expensive so they go for the church one. Many have been married civilly but not religiously, or in church, so they want to fix it up. A couple who had five children, were getting married but the man had cut himself. The poor creature had walked miles and he looked green. I would say he was suffering from blood poisoning because he showed us the cut on his leg which had become infected. Nevertheless there was great singing and clapping after the wedding took place, as well as during the ceremony.

The next day we headed off about the same time. This time to a completely different community, again in the interior. The roads to these places, often driving through fields, are rough narrow roads with huge holes in them and bridges just a couple of planks. It was really into the jungle and it felt like that for me being a newcomer.

On Saturday we set off and half way there we saw a young couple with two children and all their belongings. The man was cycling and he had all the belongings that the children would need for a full day. He had them on the back of the bike so we stopped and took the two children and all the clothes so that the couple could cycle on their own. They just had one bike. The woman was walking carrying a child. They have no prams here, so you see them carrying children for miles. We took the children and they screamed the whole way, being separated from the parents. The parents finally arrived. It was miles to this community. We arrived there and we didn't do anything in the morning, except visiting the people in the area. They lived in palha houses; palm leaf roofs and wooden sides on to them. They are all just in a small area with a church hall in the centre.

We arrived there and visited a lady who was blind and deaf. She had a forty year old mentally handicapped daughter, but as well as that, she had a huge growth in the centre of her stomach. They had brought her to Araguaina to a hospital there, but she really needed to go to Goiania where the better hospitals are. And Goiania from where they lived would be 22 hours on the bus and of course it is very expensive as well, although most Brazilians travel everywhere on the bus – which usually offers an excellent service. There were ten baptisms in the afternoon and two weddings. These communities, Sister Leonora was telling me, have Mass five times a year but they meet every week for a service.

I spent the week there and then on the Sunday I went with the Kennedy community on the back of a lorry – fifty of us were going to a place called Valley de Juari where ninety five families had finally gained access to their land. They had been put off it after people had been killed. This area is famous for big farmers putting small farmers off the land because they don't have any rights. They are unable to read or write so they have no papers, and no one has a right to the land because the landowners know more and they have money and they can buy their way in. So these families stick together, and were having a celebration. They were having Mass. There were three hundred people in solidarity, celebrating the fact that after a lot of struggle and pain and killing, they had finally gained access to the land.

We left Kennedy. I was up at half past two and we left at about four o'clock. Fifty of us on the back of a lorry, everybody singing. We let off fire crackers. When Brazil is playing football and they win, we often hear fire crackers going off, so at four o'clock in the morning to celebrate this great occasion we let off our own crackers.

We headed to a place called Juari which is about three hours, two hours of it by dirt road. We then all met in Colinas, a place where an Irish Redemptorist Priest had been on the run and had risked his life. He had worked for this community over the years in their struggle. We all met there and everybody went, one lorry after the other, till we got to Juari. I had already been there so I knew what to expect. The people seem to live in the middle of the jungle, but they have cleared away and grown corn, rice and beans, things that they needed for their families and it is fantastic to see, after a year how these things have grown, after really hard work. We arrived and met on the side of the dirt road. There were holes in the road. This was where all these families had started off trying to get the land. One of the men had been shot by a man just at random. He shot this man for no other reason than that he was on a piece of land. The mother was there with a wreath and it was really sad seeing her.

We stopped at different places along the road until we actually met at the school where we had Mass. There was hymn singing and we carried banners. We stopped at the place where the man had been shot dead. His brother gave a testimony of how he was shot. The bishop presented the mother with a wreath. It was laid on the cross, just a simple wooden cross on the side of the road. Some of the big farmers had tried to put these people off by burning out their homes. One of the crosses that they carried on the pilgrimage had been charred – really two pieces of wood from one of the houses. It was very moving to see this happening. We then met about lunch time for the Mass which finally took place, and at the offertory everybody came with gifts from the land. It was fantastic. It was so crowded and so hot, but at least we were under the shade of the hut and of all the tools they use for planting. The daughter of the man who had been killed, sowed seeds right by the cross to signify new life. That was a very moving part of the ceremony. Then we had all different kinds of talks, speeches being made, political and otherwise. We had a shared lunch. This consisted of huge pots of rice with chicken, beans and salad. People came and helped themselves. At one stage Carmen and I got really thirsty and I thought I'd love a drink of water. The water that we had brought with us had run out so we went up to one of these families and asked for some. Out of the well came the bucket with very cloudy water, unfiltered, but at that stage I couldn't have cared what it was, as long as I had liquid. We both drank the water and then the lady made coffee. In Brazil they call it cafezinho. Two mouthfuls of black sugared, very sweet coffee and that is very popular in Brazil. When you go visiting families they love to offer you this, although a lot of the families could not afford coffee.

We left about three o'clock and I came back on a covered truck because I was going back to my own community. I had finished my estagio. My time with the Brazilian community had ended. There were bumps and we were red with dust - clothes, mouths, eyebrows because the road was so dry. But we got back first, or nearly first, back to Colinas, the Irish Redemptorist house. The heavens opened as we got back which meant all the lorries coming behind us had got caught in the rain and they had no covering over the trucks. A lorry had jack-knifed on the road because of the mud so all the lorries were trapped behind it and they were soaking. When we got to Colinas we made strong coffee but they did not drink it because they were afraid to drink something hot when they were so cold. They wanted to continue as they were, soaked to the skin. Then someone had a bright idea: 'Let's have some pinga'. Pinga here is a drink, made with rum and it's lovely. It was the first drink I had here, when I arrived. It's made up of lime, sugar and pinga. Pinga is made from sugar cane. It's the local rum and it's what people can afford to drink around this area. It's very potent and a lot of people are alcoholics because of it.

This was passed around to warm their innards. All you could see was the back of the lorry, rain lashing down, thunder and lightning everywhere. This bottle was being passed from one to another, everybody taking a mouthful. One person had to be taken off the lorry, just from pure shock, tiredness and cold. We had to take her to the hospital. The thunder and lightning continued and that was how the day ended, but it was fantastic.

Each day I try to visit families here. Some of the families are very poor but coming into Colmeia you see good tarmac roads, trees lining the centre and lovely lighting. There is no electricity system and there is no water in the town. The Mayor did this in order to get votes but he has since died. People voted for him but he didn't do some of the side streets, they are still in a poor condition. They are pure dust with a big drain in the middle. Some of the people on the outskirts of the town are very poor.

An example of this was, last Saturday when we had a young child come here to say that her mother was ill and she could not afford to buy medicines. Carmen and I went off on the back of the bike and bought food stuffs. We arrived and lying on the floor on a piece of sponge was this young woman. She had a tiny sheet round her and for her pillow she had her own clothes and her children's clothes and there was nothing in the house. There was a door, the bottom half of the door was wood that had just rotted. There wasn't even a chair to sit down on. I had to go next door to get water to boil to make some soup for her. I would say a lot of her problem was just hunger. She was so delighted to receive this soup. I had put an egg in it. A lot of the neighbours gathered when we arrived so they all came in and had soup. The Brazilians have caipiras which are little stoves which are in every house, open stoves. They make their beans and rice and everything on them. That's what they boil the water on but it was very dark because they did not have any electricity. No electricity in that part of town. It was just a joy to see that creature have some soup, something to eat. I went down yesterday, Saturday morning at nine o'clock to a catechism group that meet under a mango tree. There was the mother and her two children who were having catechism lessons. She came to pick them up. So it was great to see her well again. That's the type of families/people you come across, day in day out. Yet on the other side you have some very well off people.

We had First Communions last night in the church at half past seven. The priest comes once a month: 64 children, a lot of them wearing white dresses, ones that they can wear again. A lot of them were dressed up. Some people can afford it but the majority cannot. The singing was fantastic. I was playing the guitar, with two other guitarists. A man was meant to be there, who plays the accordion; he is brilliant, but didn't turn up. None of them have any musical training. There is a group of catechists in the town and they organised everything: they introduced the Mass, called the people forward for whatever it was. This is what I find fantastic that we go away for weekends and the lay people just carry on. There are four groups for liturgy. There's the Catechist group, the Charismatics, the Youth and the other group called the Apostleship of Prayer, the Apostolados. And those four groups of people take a week to organise the liturgy. They meet and pray about it and decide what they are going to do. We don't always give the homily at all, far from it. As I said we have been away for the past three weekends so the people just gave the homily and organised everything.

We have leaders' meetings and we invite people to come up and use the books that we have here for helping them with their homilies. Some of them do this. But they are fantastic at standing up and leading. A young couple stands up, there are about twenty people, for example in the Charismatic group, and eighteen in the Youth, and they introduce the service. We only have Mass once a month, so the group who is on that week organise the Mass but otherwise the people do the services themselves. It's great when you go out to the communities to see this happen.

Before I came here I read Clodovis Boff's book, "Feet on the Ground Theology" It's his diary of five months he spent here in the interior, further north of here, six months he spent lecturing in theology in Rio de Janeiro. He writes about his experiences, the long walks he does, the people coming for the cultos, for the services. He recounts what we have done to people once the priest or the sister arrives. They automatically want us to take over. So we try when we go out just to do the little bit of chipping in when necessary, but the people continue to lead as they always lead without our presence.

We went to one community in my first week here and nobody had been there for a month. We went out on a Saturday evening and it was really dark. The Brazilian priest was coming for his once a year Mass. He was meant to come at half past two and the Mass was meant to be at four o'clock. He did not arrive until four o'clock. The people walked miles to get there and Mass did not begin until half past five. The leader of the community asked if we would go out with the priest to bless his little piece of farm land, and he was so thrilled because he had corn growing and vegetables. So we set off. We have an old Volkswagon here which we use for trips to the interior and for journeys if we are doing courses. Normally around town I use the bike – I go out every day on the bike – or just walk. This time we drove to see his piece of land and to bless it. There wasn't a road, a mule had been on it before and there were huge stones everywhere. We have a special iron plate underneath the Volks to take us, because we were on these journeys thumping on the ground. The Brazilian priest kept saying 'Meu Deus, My God, My God!' We drove over a river. We drove through part of a river, as there was no crossing at all. Margie kept saying 'My God'. While the driver kept telling us 'it is very near pertinho', which means 'it's right beside us'. It was in fact miles away. So we had to use the lights to get back as it was just getting dark. I became quite scared because of the planks on the small bridges.

I arrived on 31st August and I drove about a week after from the Sertao on one of the dirt tracks. I had just got my license. My Brazilian license which lasts me for a few months and then I get it for three years. Next week we will be going to Miracema which is where the bishop lives, and we have a meeting of all the people who are full time leaders, lay leaders, religious and priests for a big assembly.

We had a meeting there with Maria Teresa last week, one of the counsellors who had come out from Ireland. The Centre is a retreat house and also a seminary for young Brazilian priests. The seminary is right on the edge of the Tocantins River. It is a beautiful, lovely setting. You can see the river and the ferries going across, boats going up and down the river, and people washing, both themselves and their clothes in the river.

Most people in Brazil have a roca, their little garden with their vegetables in it. So I decided I'd have ours growing here. I visited this Brazilian community. I got cabbage plants and I got all kinds of herbs and growing things, although our soil is very bad, stones, and not rich in nutrients at all. So I planted cabbages, which are growing beautifully, as well as spring onions, green onions and garlic. The Brazilians love garlic: garlic in everything. In fact one of the cures for worms here is three cloves of garlic first thing in the morning in milk. So I have had a couple of sessions of that for three mornings in a row. I've also planted beetroot, lettuce, tarragon, cilantro and different kinds of herbal teas. Most people around here use them in fact they go around selling them. They are keeping me going. The mums here say I should get my wheelbarrow out and go on the streets to sell these to earn my keep.

I go for some Portuguese lessons with a young mother who is expecting her second child in January. She wants to learn some English and I want to learn Portuguese so we do an exchange. I go to her in the mornings. I'm glad to have something structured. Afternoons, I go visiting. Then we have a time of prayer together. We have the Eucharist and we pray sitting out in the area at the back of the house which looks into the valley with palm trees and mountains away in the distance. Our house is in a lovely setting in Colmeia because we are up on a hill. The tarmac road ends here, so any communities we visit after that further west of here towards the River Araguaia are via all dirt roads. The road was meant to be tarmac five/six years ago but money ran short. That's the story of so many projects that take place here. Another one was in Pedro Afonso another town on the river, the River Tocantins. They started building a huge bridge, they built the two columns either side. The guy who was up for election didn't get in so the project was abandoned. Two huge columns built and no bridge. Money squandered. The people who are at the top use the money for anything but what they're meant to be using it for. You have all these kinds of stories and the poor remain poor.

At Christmas time, we have a meeting down in Goiania, our community in the south. That's twenty hours by bus from here. We will stay in our community there. We have a meeting and a one day retreat, with reflections: a Brazilian nun will come in to speak to us and the rest of the time we have meetings. After Christmas, this year, in the state of Goias our state was divided in two, and the capital at the moment is Miracema but in about ten years time there is going to be a new capital called Palmas. At the moment it's a village alongside the river with about three houses. So there's going to be a city built. Where the money is coming from is a mystery. One of the mayor's sons has gone off to Paris and to London to see how cities are built. We have extremes, it's unbelievable. We hope to go to Goiania which is the city of well over a million people down in the south of the state. The heat there is oppressive. I stayed there in the month of August and we travelled into town for meetings. The buses are full, morning, noon and night. It's a pushing match to get on to them as there's no such thing as a queue. Everybody gets onto the bus at the same time, so it's every person for themselves. You become like the natives, if you stood back you'd never get onto the bus.

We have all kinds of tarantulas: huge spiders, just as the rainy season begins. We're beside a farm and also beside a grass area. So these animals keep coming into the room because there is a space under the door. I have had huge tarantulas up my wall. One night I was going to turn the pump on for water and I almost stepped on a scorpion. That terrified me. One night I don't know why, I woke up at half past twelve. Everybody has mosquito nets over their beds and I was tucked in under mine. I keep my torch under my pillow because I have no bedside lamp. I sat up in bed, bolt upright and shone the torch round thinking there was a spider. I just got this feeling there was something in the room. I shone it on the wall and at the door. Just before I was getting back under the bedclothes I shone the torch at the side of my bed: there was a snake crawling through my flip flops. It was crawling through the middle of one of them. I froze, I was just terrified. I tore a hole in my net in my haste to get out quickly and put the light on to see what this animal was. I ran next door to Carol. "Carol there's a snake in my room". She courageously killed the snake. Since then I have the bottom half of my door sealed off. It was just a one off thing that would never happen again. At least they kept re-assuring me that it had never happened before and probably won't again. I take precautions all the same.

Here in Brazil, especially in the interior, there is a whole group of the churches called Assembleia de Deus, the Assembly of God: they meet every night to pray and thump the Bible. They denounce Catholics and are called 'Crentes' here. The women have to wear their hair in a bun. They mustn't drink or smoke or dance. They wear their sleeves long and even the men have to wear their shirt sleeves long. They have a great hold on a lot of the poor people here and in the small villages. As for working together, it is unheard of. There's a Menonite group here, and we have had a lot of contact with *them*. The couple are American, they've been up to visit and we've been down to them. There's no problem. We've got Baptists and Methodists here in the town, but the bigger group are these fundamentalists.

Here we have a Novena nine days before Christmas, people come and pray in the church every night. Last night for First Communion, they decorated the church with flowers, ferns on every seat. I thought it was really beautiful, that the fact they just use nature here – everything that's growing. Christmas is not a big event. The biggest event here in Brazil is the Carnival. We arrived the night before, last year, in Rio. It wasn't the best of nights to arrive in Brazil. We didn't have any bother as we arrived so late at night and the celebration night was almost over.

This coming Sunday we have our Parish Council meeting which begins at 12.00 and will probably end around 4pm. All the leaders from the communities come to it so the material they need for the Christmas novena can be given to them. There can be up to 40 people at it and my memory of the last one was that of a terrible heat as we were in the Parish hut and it has an asbestos roof. Fortunately the sides are open. The Christmas novena begins on the 14th December and is held in the various sections of the town. The leaders organise nine houses in their area for it each evening and on the last night all come to Church carrying lighted candles for the final celebrations. It's a big occasion for the Brazilians.

We had some terrible incidents in the town last week. A parishioner, well known and loved, was shot dead at the local petrol station by three hired gunmen (called pistoleiros). They got away but were caught crossing a bridge to the next state, brought back here and put in gaol at the end of the town. We went down to lead prayers and to sympathise with the widow. However the next morning we discovered that the widow had hired the gunmen: she and her mother had planned it. The police do nothing here, so the men of the town decided to show the other towns in the area, that Colmeia would not tolerate gunmen, so they stormed the prison, forty of them and beat to death the three gunmen. Nobody could stop them. They left their bodies lying in the street; it was just awful. Now since then, we've heard that the families of the gunmen want to take revenge and so the people here are very fearful and lorry loads of families left town at the weekend. Fortunately they are now back again. Margie led the funeral service for the man who had been shot and the Church was packed. The bodies of the gunmen were taken back to the state where they had come from.

Today is Sunday and we're celebrating the feast of the Ascension. This morning at 8.00am I went to a very poor part of the town to see how two new young catechists were getting on with their class. It was held outside and there were all ages at it. They had prayers, a short Bible reading and games. Then at 9 am I came back to the Church for 11 baptisms. A team of four lay people and Margie as Parish co-ordinator, run the course and then do the baptisms. Here godparents are very important people so they wait months or years sometimes for them to arrive here. It is compulsory that the parents and godparents do a two day course beforehand. Last Saturday and yesterday were the course days, then the baptisms were today. I helped with the team and actually did the baptisms – my only difficulty was getting my tongue around some complicated names.

A couple of weeks ago a group of catechists from here went out to one of the communities to take the confirmation class. I was going as musician and was in the back of the lorry with about ten others plus produce they had bought in town. Half way there on the dirt road we got a flat tyre. When we all got off they discovered they had no jack, so they got stones and trees and hoisted the lorry on to a tank of gas. I was terrified it would explode. Some cars and lorries are run on gas. We set off again and there was a terrible noise and it was discovered that the nuts on the wheel weren't the right ones, so we all got off again. The same happened again but finally they got it fixed. Meanwhile some of us started walking. This was at 10am and the sun was beating down on us. We eventually got to the farm and everyone helped to prepare lunch –

rice, beans and pork. The farm had trees laden with tangerines, oranges, bananas and lemons so we helped ourselves to fruit and then drove to the centre for the class. It was 1pm, the hottest part of the day. The centre has just wooden sides and an asbestos roof – asbestos is used a lot here. I didn't think they've heard of the serious illness "asbestosis". I know that asbestos is banned in England. For here the asbestos roofing is so hot – you can feel the heat on your head. We had a creamery can of water and gallons were drunk before the class ended at 4pm. We taught them some new hymns and the catechists from Colmeia took the class. The young people are so simple and eager to hear and listen. I marvel at their powers of listening, especially in the heat, as I am usually wilting in the background. We did not get back until 6pm after a really good day. I enjoy these visits to the centre, some 18 kilometres from here.

Last Sunday the Youth, who meet every Sunday from 9 – 11am, decided to have a fun day and walk to a nearby farm, so we all set off at 6am! We cheated and got a lift in a lorry but walked back in the afternoon at 4pm. They carried rice, saucepans, a chicken, in fact everything. They killed two more chickens for the lunch. Everything was washed in the river. They used 14 kilos of rice. It was relaxing and they enjoyed it. They sang, danced, prayed and played.

This reminds me, since the middle of April I go walking every morning with a group of women from the town. We get up at 5am and collect the others on route – some mornings there's a big group, other days only four of us. It is a good way for me to learn the language and to know what's happening too, although half the time I switch off and just watch the stars, as it is dark when we set off. We are back around 6.30am, enjoying by then, the warm air.

I visit the hospital now on a regular basis – it is so small and cramped and hygiene doesn't exist. I just hope I don't have to go in there for anything. Two weeks ago a small baby was there suffering from being given too many medicines. The people just don't know and go off to the chemist and are given a bottle. They feel the 'bought' is better than the natural. Anyway the poor wee baby died. I went down to its home, a very poor family, and in one tiny room there were men making the coffin. It was so sad. They lined it with a sheet and a few white ribbons and that was it. The poor here just use very light coffins, wood and cloth. The close relatives don't usually go to the grave on the funeral day, they wait until the 7th day when they bring candles, a simple wooden cross and flowers and things to plant.

The theme of our Lenten campaign is "solidarity in the dignity of work". I'm sorry to be going away from the parish during Lent as weekly meetings are planned, and when I planned this retreat last June I wasn't involved, and it never occurred to me that it was Lent. However before I'd left I'd taught all the Lenten hymns in the Parish and in various communities. We send tapes out and song sheets but when communities have no electricity and only a few can read it's a different story. For this reason a lot of Brazilian hymns have the repetition of last lines and choruses.

Yesterday I went off on the back of Fr. Joe's motor bike to see where he lives and works. Two of them, Redemptionists, live among the people in the same type of mud house. It is simple living, using water from a barrel for a shower. When I arrived, all the kids came in and we sang the Lenten hymn. Joe has a guitar so I got handed it. Then we set off for a Bible circle meeting but that had been cancelled, which was a pity. I visited a couple of families and then went to a fish restaurant; the most delicious fish and we were overlooking two rivers. Unfortunately I was almost eaten alive with mosquitoes, which I can never manage to escape.

We had our Diocesan planning meeting to plan our year's work. All the priests, religious and three lay people from each parish came to it. We looked at our Diocesan priorities and planned accordingly. This year we're hoping to have an auxiliary Bishop as Don Jaime was 70 last week and has had two major heart surgeries. Seven parishes are run by priests and eight by sisters in the diocese, which is about the size of Ireland. In Colmeia we had our own Parish planning meeting for the year with all the leaders from each sector present. Then we had to go out to the other towns and do the same. Last Sunday we had four communities in the interior come together for a Lenten meeting and to learn some hymns. It was held outside under a mango tree. This was much cooler than in a small school building. I was leading the hymns and in the middle of singing a lady came in with a tin can of drinking water and offered it around.

The health programme is under way again with four new leaders. Even with this, three babies have died over the past month in Colmeia. We send off a report to a central organisation in Southern Brazil regarding babies weights and causes of death. I am learning patience. I could take the forms home and fill them in myself in half an hour but that would not benefit the group. Some of the women find it difficult just to count the numbers together. We're working too with the local health post, and the nurses there are willing to come and talk to the groups on hygiene and vaccinations.

In Colmeia we've started to build a church after an 8year struggle with the Prefect (Mayor). Everything here has political implications and over the past years there were rows between the Prefect and us. Things have been resolved and now the building has begun. We have a novena of our patron saint at the end of July until 6th August, 9 nights of novena and a festa afterwards to make money. At this, cakes, chicken, cheese and other items of food will be auctioned. The finance committee had gone out to some of the big farmers to ask for their calves. Some of these large farm owners have huge areas of land but don't live there. They have houses in Sao Paulo and fly up and down from there.

Our dry season is here, which brings a cool breeze in the mornings but terrible heat in the afternoons. For the farmers it is the time to 'burn' their land and have it ready for the rainy season and time of planting. I can see fires in the distance – smoke everywhere and when travelling on the main high way the long dry grass at the sides of it is on fire.

Last Friday Ann, a young mother and her four year old and myself, set off for a hospital in Baum that specialises in operations for the deaf and for children with hair-lips. I made the appointment for this child in May, she is deaf and cannot talk so needs a hearing aid and to be taught to talk. It is a fantastic hospital and the staff were lovely. Because Perlare, the 4 year old, had wax in one ear they weren't able to finish the tests so we have to come back in November and stay one week. We left Friday at 9pm and arrived Sunday at 3pm, a very long trip. Then afterwards the mother and child returned to Colmeia and then I came on into Sao Paulo, 4 hours from the hospital which is in the state of S. Paulo. This city is so big 18-20 million people, huge buildings and constant pollution. We're staying with Jimmy, an Irish priest. I did the language course with him. His parish has 200,000 living mainly in favelas and it's a one and a half hour ride from the bus station. This weekend we hope to visit the Maryknolls and other groups working here, then we hope to spend a few days by the sea in a lovely spot between S. Paulo and Rio. It is cold here and I have socks and shoes on for the first time since last year.

We're organising the Christmas novena. Yesterday we had a Parish Assembly for the whole day, Sunday, and each leader brought three persons from their sector or community. New directives have been brought out by the Brazilian Bishops for the next four years. Part of the day was to study this document. We did this at Diocesan level and the feed back was given to the Parish yesterday. All this was interspersed with songs and learning new ones. We have decided to leave Colmeia at the end of 1992, a decision that wasn't too easy to make. We told the Bishop and people some weeks ago and gave our reasons. We feel we should move to a needier area, as here the leaders are well formed and can carry on without us.

Yesterday we organised the Assembly with the lay leaders and they did it all. It was great to see this. It means more work and meetings but worth it in the end. It also needs a lot of patience, the people take their time getting through the agenda: I could have done it in half of the time. I'm learning so much about patience, the need to sit around, chat and wait, and then the action happens after this.

The Bishop, a Kerry man, wasn't too pleased at our decision to leave. However we are looking at the other areas in the Diocese and outside the Diocese. We want to continue to work in the interior as there's a big plea from the workers in the interior. In this new state of Tocantins a new city is being built from scratch and people are flocking there for work. Last year in one village there were 2,000 inhabitants, this year there are 60,000 people. Mobility is part of the Brazilian lifestyle, and they think nothing of just getting up and moving overnight. Maybe we can learn something here.

I did a funeral the other day of an old lady whom I visited many times. She suffered so much and in such terrible conditions. Health Care is nil in such circumstances. She was buried in a cloth coffin. Part of the ritual when the body was being taken out of the house was to sweep the floor and then they threw the dust after the coffin when the lorry was taking it to the graveyard. They also threw the broom out of the door into the drain. The funeral day is not that important – the seventh day is the day when all the relatives go to the graveyard and plant flowers and put candles all round the grave and put up a simple cross. In other areas they have a Mass but here we have a service in the graveyard. The other day when I was with the family we began at 3.30 and ended around 6pm. All the old ladies chanted litanies.

Here we are beginning our New Year with all kinds of planning meetings. Our diocesan one is next week when we plan the year's work together: six from each parish will participate. We've just had our health programme and elected two new co-ordinators. It's only in its second year and patience is the name of the game.

It's raining here non-stop for three days and in other parts of Brazil there is terrible flooding. Our diocesan planning meeting may be cancelled now as the centre is built on the bank of the river Tocantins and it's rising every day. This Sunday its Baptisms. I've been doing them for the past months and there are sixteen.

I came back from home thinking that leaving Colmeia would be the only thing uppermost on my mind. I was brought back to reality very quickly when a few days after I got back, Anne who lives with me, announced that for personal reasons she was leaving. So the last few weeks have been difficult, but somehow it has brought the group closer together.

Our final Mass here is on the 27th December and we leave Colmeia on the 31st. I'll be sad leaving the people. During our meeting we decided to move to Palmas, Brazil's newest city in the interior, which is growing rapidly. In the meantime I move to Barrolandia where we have a community. In January I'll be staying with some Brazilian sisters who live near Palmas and look into buying a house there.

Chapter 4: Palmas: 1993

Bernice from Ghana and I moved to Palmas on the nineteenth of March. Palmas is the new capital of the state of Tocantins and building began three years ago. So we have people from every state in Brazil coming here in the hope of finding work. We are living on the periphery of the city in a "bairro" that is very poor. 15,000 families are there living in houses of black plastic or palm leaf. Some were lucky at the beginning to get a half-house, two rooms and a bathroom and quite a few families have this type of house. We've rented a half-house until we decide which of the three "quadras" we would live in. Each "quadra" has 5,000 families. At the moment we're doing a lot of visiting to get to know the situation here.

On our first Sunday when we arrived at the little chapel built a year ago of light wood with an asbestos roof, we were greeted with a song "Go work in the world and proclaim the Good News", and then we had to introduce ourselves. There was a poster up on the wall with our names on it. At the offertory everybody brought us fresh flowers; some were tiny posies. They stayed on afterwards to greet us. It was very moving.

I've met some people from Colmeia who have moved here too. Our main work will be 'formation of leaders'. It's challenging beginning in a new place and everybody is new to Palmas. The plan of the city is on the same lines as Brasilia with huge open spaces. I use the bike to collect our post and go to the bank, as everything is quite spread out. Some of the buildings are quite smart but there are extremes everywhere. I went up to the north east of Brazil for my retreat and this took me forty four hours by bus. The nun who led the retreat came down from the U.S.A. so it was all in English.

Bernice, from Ghana, and myself have been here in Palmas for the past three months. It feels like years as I'm that much more at home with myself and the people now. The African influence of Bernice is also helping me to look at situations differently. The first weeks I found very difficult and for me the move was like coming to Brazil all over again, but the retreat after Easter helped me to put things into perspective. This week we move into our house which will give us a little more space. We've had to replace the asbestos roof with tiles which will help to keep it cooler. It is our dry season and we're having heavy dust storms. It is what I imagine the Sahara desert to be like: dust everywhere, we're eating it!

There are three quadras here with 5,000 people in each one. Everybody here is new: when you ask 'Where have you come from?' it's usually from every state in Brazil and 'How long have you been here?' the reply is, 'One month, six months, a year or two years'. So we're all beginners. One quadra yesterday had its first Mass on a plot of land with dust blowing everywhere. Everybody stood around the altar/table.

The new city is being built in an unknown part of Tocantins in order to bring work and development to the other side of this River. It is surrounded by mountains and has some beautiful parts out in the country: you can swim in a river right in the middle of the rocks and mountains. It has huge spaces and distances. No doubt, over the years, development will take place. There are no trees planted yet and with the sun they're a must.

Right now it is pouring out of the heavens so I've a chance to do my Christmas mail. Our rains have come very late this year. We had a great victory when 1,200 families received their own plot of land on which to build their house/hut. These families were living in absolute misery, in terrible conditions on top of one another. Now they have at least a dignified open space around them. We're continuing to struggle for better housing, light and water and sanitation for the families. On the day before one of these groups was to move, a fire broke out in one of the straw huts and within twenty minutes around 200 families lost everything, the little they had. It was the most terrifying experience of my life, it was an absolute miracle that no one died, a few had burns and one woman got quite badly burned. There were tanks of gas exploding everywhere. Within hours people came in droves to give food, clothing and shelter to these families. The generosity of people was incredible. We spent a week sorting out clothing and shoes to give to the families who had lost everything.

Next year in Palmas we're having a Mission: it was meant to be in Lent but had been put off until June '95. The launching of this Mission is on Christmas night and we are having a lot of pre-mission meetings with bishops and many religious congregations who are all involved in it. Our Parish stretches for 300kms so there's a huge area to be covered. Right now we're having our Advent meetings and planning for the Christmas novena.

We have seen many changes and participated in many events here in Palmas. One of the big moments for us was the mission that we had been preparing for, for over a year. Around 72 people, bishops, priests, lay people and sisters came from other parts to help with the actual mission. Each community was asked to do something concrete at the end of the mission. One community chose to build a house for a lady who is both deaf and dumb. The idea was that the community would choose something they would all do together. Some collected wood and nails, while others made a meal for the workers. The deaf and dumb lady was absolutely thrilled with her wooden home.

Another moment for us, as a Congregation, happened one Saturday night when Elenice, our first Brazilian sister made her final vows. The whole parish participated in this event offering hospitality to those who travelled from far away places. The Mass itself was really lovely, and her mother, brother and sisters travelled long distances to be with Elenice for this event.

This concludes extracts from Katey's letters. What follows is an account of Father Kenneth Payne's subsequent visit to Brazil.

Chapter 5: Visiting Palmas: 1998

Five years after, I had the opportunity for seeing for myself something of the life in Palmas. Katey met me at the airport and drove me to the bungalow where she lived. The land round where she lived in Palmas was fairly flat, quite overgrown with green shrubs and all sorts of plants and areas which had been carved out of the scrubland for the building of very simple dwellings. Some of the settlers had been there since about 1989 and they were in more established areas with concrete roads quite pleasantly laid out. However, most of the people were unemployed and had come in from all over Brazil in order to find work. Very often they began in wooden plastic huts and then gradually improved their situation by gathering together enough bricks to build some sort of dwelling. But much of the land was still divided up by earth roads, which after a shower of rain became soft with mud. The Sisters' bungalow was situated between a Pentecostal church and a café, Bunny's Bar, which seemed continually to be polluting the atmosphere with a very loud ghetto-blaster. I had no sooner had a quick bite to eat when we went off to a Penitential service, which was run by two of the priests from the parish. The parish was divided into eleven communities, each community living in a designated area in what was until recently shrub land. The service was led by lay people while two priests heard confessions outside the very rough and primitive hut which passes for a church.

The next morning, Palm Sunday, we were up, as every morning, early and joined the procession which began at 7.30 am when the temperature was already nearly 30°c. We wound our way through several of the Christian communities waving palms and branches from the undergrowth, singing, pausing to listen to passages read from the Passion of Jesus, and gathering up more people at each stop. We passed dwellings of varying degrees of dereliction and poverty until we finally ended beneath a lean-to roof on the side of a school building. I remained amongst the congregation whilst Padre Pedro, a long-haired Brazilian priest in his thirties, together with two others, prepared to continue the celebration of the Mass.

Then, to my amazement, I realised that Padre Pedro was beckoning to me to come up to the altar and join him in concelebrating. With some hesitation, I complied, and no one seemed to worry that I suddenly appeared with the others, but, unlike them, I was just wearing trousers and a short-sleeved shirt by then soaked in sweat for it was approaching midday. I joined in a part of the Eucharistic prayer in English, and immediately Mass was over many of the crowd came up to us, warmly and unselfconsciously embracing us, the children hugging and kissing us. I could not but reflect what the reaction to this would be in England with its present concern regarding paedophilia.

The Sisters' bungalow comprised three very small bedrooms, together with an equally small but adequate kitchen, shower room, and all this giving on to a central sitting and eating area. When the Sisters moved in the roof was of corrugated iron but they improved it by having it tiled. However, there was no ceiling, and when lying in bed I perceived daylight through the pats in the tiles, and one night there was a storm, which even the local people considered to be one of the worst they had known. The thunder, God's ghetto-blaster, made the noise from Bunny's Bar seem a mere whisper, and the spray coming in through the roof made the morning shower almost superfluous.

The two Sisters living there, in a multitude of ways, helped and inspired by the various Christian communities around them, ran an important healing centre. These flourish throughout Brazil and the Sisters see their role as instigating them, and as in Rio, training local personnel to run them. I found it well equipped, with use being made of natural medicines, no drugs at all. There were natural remedies for every sort of ailment, made mostly from herbs, which grew in the wild undergrowth all around. Just a few were cultivated specially in the Sisters' tiny garden. One evening I was doing the washing up – one didn't need to know Portuguese to do that – and I threw some eggshells into the waste bin. This provoked an exclamation and a slight reprimand from Sister. Eggshells had to be washed, dried in the sun, carefully crushed to a fine powder before being used as the principal constituent in a multi-mixture for pregnant mums. This was important as so many babies were born under-nourished. The seeds and pips from various fruit were also used. It seemed that the small black seeds of papaya, crushed up are good for people with cancer.

At the centre, the Pastoral da Crianca as it was called, the elderly were also involved. I saw some lovely baskets made out of tightly rolled up pieces of newspaper varnished over, which were surprisingly seemed quite strong. There were also classes in reading and writing. However, it was the young who shone most by their involvement in all aspect of life in this poor region. Erivelton, for example, was a lad of twenty-one who had been elected leader of this Christian community. After being out of work he had recently got a job in a large store, but wanted to go on to university to read law in order to use his skill in the struggle for human rights in Brazil. In most towns human rights groups are active. Many are financed from voluntary organisations in Germany and young people, like Erivelton, are involved.

Just before I arrived, the president of the Tocantins, who had his palace in Palmas had proposed constructing a tarmacadam tree-lined avenue up to his palace. Within less than two kilometre from him there were people living in shacks by the side of muddy, potholed roads and with no electricity and no clean water. The human rights group staged a peaceful demonstration to protest about this. Often notice *was* taken by the authorities and change occurred.

The human rights group in Palmas, run by two young women with the voluntary help of a lawyer, dealt in a practical way with the problems occurring in the community. They organised educational programmes, as well as dealing with adolescent pregnant women who had been left high and dry by the man in the picture; they accompanied people who had been treated violently by the police; they ensured that a youngster of twelve was not put in with hardened criminals when put into prison; they tried to deal with the problem of street children, and glue sniffing which was rampant in the centre of Palmas and then there were small farms around Palmas and sometimes rogues came with false documents to claim the land back and so there would be a dispute as to who really had a right to the land.

However, problems with children were the most common. Some could be dangerous. Psychologists claimed, I think rightly, that the reason for so many of these problems was that many kids lacked love and a suitable occupation. It was important that moral values were passed on. Many children were high on drugs, had knives in their clothes and sometimes if teachers resisted them they would run the risk of being attacked and killed themselves. Terasina, who was a good friend of Sister Katey's and lived just round the corner from her, was a Notre Dame nun teaching in a local school, and she was trying on one occasion to negotiate between three different gangs, but had to be escorted back home at night because she was nearly killed herself.

Early one morning there was an accident just outside our bungalow. A motorcyclist had crashed over a hole in the road. He was not badly injured but had to be taken to hospital. Our concrete road had been built only a year or so previously, but the sewerage channel ran quite near the surface and at intervals there were round holes with concrete covers. However, some of these covers to the manholes had been broken, probably because they were not very well made in the first place. This was the case with the one outside and it had merely been marked in the road by a couple of pieces of wood placed over the hole. The cyclist had hit these and throughout the remainder of my stay there the sewerage welled up into the roadway: not a very healthy situation.

The last days of Holy Week and of Easter will always remain as the most memorable and meaningful of my life. The expressive and relevant liturgies, led by young people, brought the whole redemptive drama of our faith to life. This, coupled with the warmth of the welcome given to me on each occasion, although I was unable to communicate with the people in Portuguese, was unforgettable. The Way of the Cross on Good Friday, when hundreds of us walked in the heat through some of the Christian communities, stopping at crossroads, and corners to witness the re-enaction of a scene from the Passion rendered by altogether some eighty young people, dressed for the part, from Father Pedro's group brought tears to my eyes: I felt so much a part of it, and even more so when arms stretched out towards me whenever I paused to take a sip of cold water from the flask I had been advised to take with me. The Way of the Cross took nearly three hours, and well before we reached the marketplace where the crucifixion took place with Padre Pedro on the cross, my water flask was empty through having shared it with so many, and we were all thirsty with the Lord. Pedro, as he hung on the cross, added to the words of Jesus, and cried out in a loud voice that as long as we have the unemployed, as long as we have bad health care, as long as we have children suffering and people who are poor and oppressed, then Jesus will not come down from the cross. He continues to suffer in and through us.

Padre John, another priest helping in the parish, celebrated the Easter Vigil, introducing me to the people packed into the church, which held about three hundred. One man, seated near the front, immediately stood up and reiterated what Padre John had said, agreeing that everyone there was so pleased that I was with them that evening. It was so spontaneous and genuine.

A great fire was blazing outside the church and although it did not happen on this particular occasion, often each person who came would bring a piece of wood and throw it on to the fire. This symbolised their old life, their sins and failings and they were burnt to ashes by the fire. Four Easter candles were lit from the fire and they were held by members of the four different communities taking part. Lots of people brought bottles of water, which were placed on a table by the altar and were blessed during the vigil. People then took them home. As would be expected, it was a lively liturgy and several times the congregation, more or less spontaneously, sang out their joy at the Lord's Resurrection. At the end, as seemed customary, crowds of people swarmed around both Padre John and me, hugging and kissing and shaking hands, and occasionally showing off one or two words of English.

We all adjourned afterwards to Terasina's house and had a bite to eat. The night was short and Bunny's Bar had its ghetto-blaster going at its loudest and there were many people dancing outside. This was apparently very common, particularly on Holy Saturday evening. There was also a country custom whereby after midnight you could go and steal a chicken and cook it for lunch on Easter Sunday! We did in the event have chicken but I do not think it was stolen! In fact, for Easter Sunday lunch we were many kilometres distant from Palmas.

There were three rural communities, some sixty to seventy kilometres away, who had not seen a priest for about four months. Each group of Christians in these villages was held together and co-ordinated by a small community of nuns. However, in the first, at Aparecida, it would be truer to say that it was just one German Sister, Irene, who animated the Christians, and, indeed most of the thousand or so inhabitants of the village. Sister Irene possessed a strong and vibrant personality and not only held the Christian community together leading the Sunday liturgy but she also ran a vast compound for training the local people in farming techniques, fish breeding and other agricultural skills, to say nothing of lessons for children in the three R's, painting, carpentry, religious education and music. However, perhaps her greatest accomplishment had been to train a considerable number of leaders.

Some of the young people would come in from a distance of forty to sixty kilometres. In the fish reservoirs there were as many as three thousand fish and they were really the only things that made any sort of profit, although I was surprised to find that she reckoned that it was only a third self-supporting. I think this was partly because she seemed to give a lot of things away, including the meals, and the local people were unable to buy much of the produce especially the fish, which they liked, because they had no money. Furthermore, half of the proceeds of what was sold was divided amongst the children. I saw quite a lot of cocoa trees and I was given a stone to suck off the soft surround and the technique was then to put the stone out to dry and then roast it. The result would be cocoa! There were banana trees, sweetcorn and an enormous variety of other produce. There was great poverty in the village itself as those who did work were very poorly paid and sometimes the motivation in going to help Sister Irene, or going to learn something from her project, was simply in order to get a free meal. It turned out that often they had no food on Sunday when they didn't go to see her and so they were quite hungry when they turned up again on Monday.

I was with Father Matt Ryan, the Irish vice-provincial of the Redemptorists, of whom quite a few work in this part of Brazil. We celebrated the Easter Mass with Sister Irene's community of villagers, had lunch with her, and then sped to another village, Novo Accordo, where three more religious Sisters looked after the Christian community there. Another Easter Sunday Mass was celebrated before visiting a third even more rural and remote community, Novo Horizon, where Sister Madeleine, a French nun, welcomed us. She, and her companion Sister, came from near Strasbourg, but a second nun was absent in France visiting her aged mother.

The cottage in which the two Sisters lived – Madeleine actually had a friend staying there just for a short time – was only built about two years previously, and it was a fairy-tale building. The floor was concrete, the thatch was enormously thick and apparently made out of thirty thousand pieces of straw. When it rained heavily, you could hardly hear the rain: it was just a soft distant murmur, so Madeleine enthusiastically informed us. I was pleased that she was French as she was one of the few people with whom I could really communicate directly, and in consequence I learned a lot from her. The concrete floor of the cottage, as also in Katey's bungalow, and in most other places we visited, was ordinary rough concrete which was burned with a machine and through which multicolours were impregnated so that the end result was quite smooth and looked quite attractive. Both the Sisters were artistic and had made all sorts of interesting carvings and plaques from local wood, coconut shells and various products of nature. Matt was also very much at home there and we had hardly set foot in the cottage when he led me down to the stream. This was in a hollow surrounded by a great deal of vegetation and here it was that Matt had his wash in the nude, as also did the three ladies – after he had finished. I went down more modestly a little later. The only spectators to what must have been quite an amazing scene were a horse and a donkey which we passed on the way.

A further quite lively Easter Mass was celebrated there in a newly built Pastoral Centre which Madeleine was hoping to equip rather in the same way that Katey had done in her community, with alternative medicines, rooms for classes, lessons and so on. The main room was quite full for the Mass and the chairs were arranged in a semi-circle with an excellent music group, guitar, drums, and several of the youngsters dressed up in very dignified Middle-Eastern costumes to enact the Gospel of the Resurrection. Madeleine's touch was very evident in all this and the Mass was a most enjoyable event, although I felt the sweat literally running down my back and chest underneath my shirt and alb. Even the locals were commenting that it was very hot – over 40°c.

When we came out of Mass it was pitch dark and although it was only about one hundred and fifty yards to Madeleine's cottage I found it very difficult to see my way. There were, of course, no street lights. The inhabitants if they wanted to go to the bigger village, Novo Accordo, on the other side of the river, had to get a boat down or walk round the way that we had come in the car, but I gathered that was not usual.

I looked up at the stars for a long time. The quietness, the peace, and the darkness and the little cottage and the whole atmosphere of the place, together with Madeleine herself, charmed me beyond words. I was to sleep in a room, the third bedroom in the cottage, and Katey and

Gina who had come with us were to sleep in hammocks in the Pastoral Centre. I was concerned about this because I knew that neither of them would sleep very well in a hammock as they'd mentioned this to me. Also there would be no mosquito nets and that could be a problem. However, they insisted that this was how it should be and so I had a tiny room with a bed, a very hard mattress and a mosquito net. There were no inside doors in the cottage just a curtain hanging over the entrance of each of the three bedrooms. There was a main room with a table and just inside the front door a gas cooker and fridge, and opposite that, a small area which was made into a prayer room with two prayer stools and matting and a couple of focal points in the way of icons on the wall. As I was about to go into my own room I noticed on the floor by the curtain covering the doorway what I thought was a doorstop and I was about to question why there should be a doorstop rather like a toad when there was no door, when it started moving: it was a toad.

Matt opted to sleep in one of the poorest cottages in Novo Accordo. It had a mud floor and was inhabited by an elderly lady with her daughter who was paralysed and in a wheelchair. When she was eighteen years old, she had been shot in the spine by another youngster. Matt knew the family well from previous visits, and a hammock had already been hung up for him across the corner of the living space. He explained to me later that his principle, when travelling from place to place, was always to stay, not in a comfortable family dwelling, but with the poorer ones.

We made our way back the following day along the long dusty track to Palmas, and I was grateful for having experienced this excursion into the rural heart of Brazil, and of having seen the Church functioning in difficult situations and without, for most of the time, a resident priest. No sooner back in the Sisters' cottage in Palmas, than the bush telegraph must have been active, and within half an hour there were several callers. Because of the heat, the door and windows were always open, and this was, at the same time, an invitation for anyone to walk in. It made no difference if one was busy with some work or engaged in conversation, the caller would invariably enter as if it was his or her home, and often go straight to the fridge and help himself to a cold drink. Privacy, and this was even more true amongst the poor, did not exist. If one was having a meal, it was not unusual for several to come in, sit down and share what we had.

Many people would come to Sister Katey with their problems. Some wanted money or food, as unemployment was rife. Most of the population of Palmas comprised people from the very poor north-east of Brazil who had come to Palmas hoping to find work, as it was a new city, expanding all the time. Ten years previously it had a population of two thousand people, and in that time this had increased a hundredfold. Then, because of the poor living conditions, disease was common and the Sisters were, with their natural remedies, like a magnet for the sick people. However, some had to be taken down to the hospital, and I saw this happening when Katey was awakened in the early hours on one morning.

The open door, and consequent hospitality to everyone was taken for granted, and one felt that it was the Gospel being lived out at its best. Occasionally discretion would be exercised and the caller would poke his head through the open window to see, first of all, if anyone was inside. However, for those of us brought up in a different culture it could at times be quite draining and exhausting, even though, in my case, I was experiencing it for only a short while. Nevertheless, when the time came for my departure, I realised that my welcome by the people in Palmas had been so warm and genuine, that I felt a deep emptiness on leaving. It became, in a sense, a death, but gathering these happenings together has become a renewed experience, a resurrection; and I hope it will be likewise for you who have been reading it.

Conclusion

There are, then, as I have tried to show, many shades of colour in Brazil. It is not just a country of football and of carnival, it is also a country where there is extreme poverty but where the Church is coming to terms with the shortage of priests and where the laity are taking a necessary lead in forming good Christian communities. Many of these are under the guidance, as we have seen, of sisters who are giving their lives in helping and training lay people to take on these responsibilities. This is surely the way forward for our Church in Europe and elsewhere. Much can be learned and acted upon, and this is in line with the thinking of Pope Francis.

Sister Katey had to terminate her work in Brazil prematurely owing to the onset of cancer, and returned to her native Ireland, dying there, with her family and friends near her on 12th April 2010. On her memorial card are the words of Saint Teresa of Avila, which sum up her spirituality:-

- "Let nothing disturb you or take away your peace, make your home in God.
- Let nothing alarm you or hold your heart in fear. Know that all things fade away.
- So be patient with what is and everything is yours, all you need your God will give.
- For with God in your heart and your faith strong in him know that you will forever live.
- Let nothing disturb you or take away your peace.

- Make your home, make your home, make your home in God."

May she rest in peace, receiving the reward of the great work she accomplished during her years in Brazil.